John Chapman

PLANTER AND PIONEER

By Ron Fridell

Illustrated by Steve Adams

Illustrated by Steve Adams

ISBN-13: 978-0-328-83284-2
ISBN-10:   0-328-83284-7

10   19

A Young Nation

John Chapman was just a little boy in the Massachusetts colony in 1776. What a great time to be alive! A new nation had just been born. It was the United States of America!

Every day that new nation grew bigger. New settlers came to America and stayed. New towns sprang up and grew. John was growing too, right along with his nation.

One morning he took a long walk. John liked wild places best. He walked deep into the wilderness. He loved the way the plants grew so thick and tangled. He loved how the wild animals hopped and flew this way and that.

"Out here a young man like me can stretch and grow," Johnny said. "The wilderness is where I belong!"

And so he would stay right there. *Now,* John thought, *what shall I do out here?*

"I will plant apple trees," he said. "Hundreds of apple trees." Of all wild plants, he loved apple trees best.

And that is what John did. He planted so many apple trees that people stopped calling him John Chapman. Now they called him Johnny Appleseed!

Let's find out more about
how John Chapman
turned into Johnny
Appleseed. It's quite a
story. It all started when
he took that walk.
And a long walk it was.

At Home Outdoors

Once John started walking, he kept walking. Every day he walked, from morning to night. He only stopped to sleep. One night he slept in a hollowed-out tree stump. The next night it was in a pile of leaves. All the day and night, summer, fall, winter, and spring, John lived outdoors.

Was John homeless? He was not. John was always at home. With all those plants and animals, he was never alone. The whole outdoors was his home!

He loved sleeping with the moon and stars above and a fire to warm him. And for food? Well, he had lots of wild fruit and vegetables. John would not go hungry.

Sometimes John had visitors. Did a man really live out here all by himself? What these visitors saw amazed them. His coat was a coffee sack with three holes. One was to poke his head through. The other two were for his arms.

The night was cold but John's feet
were bare. He said shoes hurt his feet.
He was better off without them. He
poked around the fire with a stick.

He rolled out some steaming potatoes and onions for dinner. In a little nest of leaves he had handfuls of blueberries and nuts for dessert. He had water from a nearby stream in a tin pot that he sometimes used for a hat.

"Welcome to my home," he said. "This is how I live in my wilderness. The wilderness is my home."

From Apples to "Appleseed"

John lived on the frontier. Most of the land to the west of where John had been born was wild. Out here, everybody loved apple cider. That was the juice squeezed out of apples. And no wonder. Besides water, there was hardly anything else to drink out on the wild frontier.

So John went to one of the places where cider was made. It was called a cider mill. Horses pulled big stone wheels over the apples, and out came the juice. Then the workers threw the seeds away.

Apple seeds are where apples come from. Plant an apple seed. Wait a long while. What do you get? With sun and rain, you get an apple tree. Plant a hundred seeds and what do you get? A hundred trees! So John collected hundreds of seeds. Now he could plant those apple trees. But where would he plant them?

John thought a while. Of course! He would plant them in the wild. No one had settled there yet. But they would one day. Sure, there were dangers out there. There were venomous snakes and wild wolves. But that wouldn't stop the settlers. They were looking for new places to build houses and start a new life.

They needed open places to plant fruit and vegetables and raise cows and horses. Apple trees were always a welcome sight. If he could find the right spots to plant his trees, people would come to those places. And the new nation would grow.

So John went out looking. When he found a good place, he dug holes and placed an apple seed in each one. Then he pushed the dirt back into the hole with his bare foot.

After a long day of planting many apple seeds, John slept beneath the moon and stars. The next day he walked on, looking for more good spots to plant his seeds.

He planted them along rivers and streams. He planted them in places where people would like to live. He planted hundreds of seeds. Thousands!

Soon, people stopped calling him John. Now they called him by his new name: Johnny Appleseed.

A Simple Life

Later on, Johnny returned to see how his plants were doing. He made fences from brush and fallen logs to keep wild animals away. Soon the seeds grew into small trees called seedlings.

By the time new settlers came along, they found apple trees right there waiting for them. The settlers paid money to Johnny for the land and trees. Then they built homes to stay in. And every new home helped the United States grow.

Everyone agreed that Johnny was a clever man. This Johnny Appleseed knew right where new settlers wanted to live. And those apple trees were oh so pretty! No wonder people settled down to stay.

People also liked Johnny for his energy. Was there ever a man who worked harder? He walked hundreds of miles to do all that planting.

He was one of the first planters
to bring apple trees to many states,
including Ohio, Indiana, Illinois, and
Pennsylvania. Johnny owned lots of
land and even made some money.

And what did Johnny do with this money? Did he build a big house and sit back and relax? He did not. Johnny Appleseed's home was still the great outdoors. He still ate wild fruits and vegetables. He still built fires to cook his food and keep him warm. And he still slept out beneath the moon and stars.

And why not? Nature kept giving Johnny all he needed to live his simple life. A meal of honey, fruit, berries, and cornmeal mush cooked in his tin pot was plenty.

Sometimes he would eat a meal as the guest of a frontier family. But when they led him to a soft, warm bed, he often said, "Well, no thanks." He would rather sleep under the moon and stars.

Johnny Appleseed got cold sometimes. Most of his clothes were thin and tattered. But no one ever heard him say "Poor me." Even when he did have good clothing, he would likely give it to someone who needed it more than he did. Johnny Appleseed believed that you should be thankful for whatever you had.

A Legend Is Born

The more people heard about Johnny Appleseed, the more they liked him. They heard stories that made Johnny sound like a hero. There was the time he freed a wild wolf from a trap in the woods. After that, the wolf was Johnny's friend forever.

Now, wild animals are not very friendly with people. But the wild wolf in the story stayed at Johnny's side to protect him from danger. Could that really happen? Or does it sound too good to be true?

Then there was the night when he planned to sleep in a hollow log. He looked inside and a bear was sleeping with her cubs. So Johnny left them alone. He slept out on the snow. It was cold out there. But Johnny did not want to wake them up.

And there was the time Johnny saw that sparks from his fire were killing mosquitoes. So Johnny put out the fire. Even the smallest of creatures should not be harmed, he said.

These stories may not all be true. But they show what people thought of Johnny Appleseed. They heard that he was kind to animals. So in their stories they made him super-kind. So kind that a wild wolf would stay at his side. Maybe the story was too good to be true. But that was how people wanted to remember Johnny.

They also knew that he was strong and full of energy. So they told stories that made him sound like a superman. In one story he could chop wood twice as fast as any man. In another he could walk for miles barefoot on frozen rivers. And he once jumped so high that it took him a whole day to come back down to earth.

All kinds of people told stories about Johnny Appleseed that made him sound like a hero. And a lot of people believed them. Now, put all these stories together and what do you get? Well, you get a legend. You get a man who is stronger, kinder, and smarter than any man who ever walked the earth. That was how people saw Johnny Appleseed. And that's how they wanted to remember him.

The real Johnny Appleseed died
in March of 1845 at the age of 71.
But Johnny Appleseed's legend lives on.